DATE DUE

GAYLORD			PRINTED IN U.S.A.

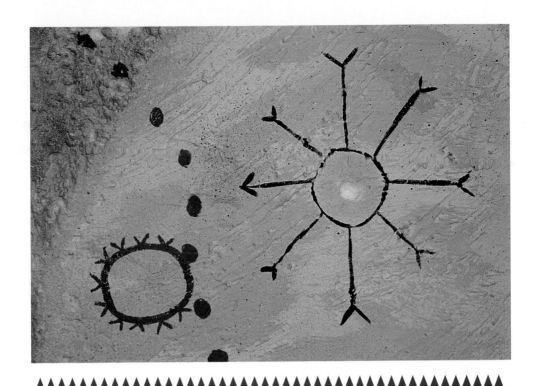

LIFEWAYS

The Chumash

RAYMOND BIAL

BENCHMARK BOOKS

MARSHALL CAVENDISH
NEW YORK

SERIES CONSULTANT: JOHN BIERHORST

ACKNOWLEDGMENTS

The Chumash would not have been possible without the generous help of a number of individuals and organizations. I would like to thank everyone at the Santa Ynez Reservation for allowing me to make photographs in the community. I would like to especially thank Susie Harrison for her assistance during my visit to California. I would like to express my deep appreciation to Dr. Robert "Nighthawk" Vann and Stuart "Proud Eagle" Grant for graciously allowing me to photograph many of the impressive objects at the Chumash Interpretive Center and Museum in Thousand Oaks. I would also like to acknowledge the many wonderful people who made our trip to California such a pleasant and memorable experience.

I would like to thank my editor Christina Gardeski for her thorough review of this manuscript. I am once again indebted to John Bierhorst for his careful reading and many helpful suggestions. As always, I offer my deepest appreciation for my wife Linda and my children Anna, Sarah, and Luke for their support of the research, writing, and photography for this book.

Benchmark Books
Marshall Cavendish
99 White Plains Road
Tarrytown, New York 10591-9001
www.marshallcavendish.com
Text copyright © 2004 by Raymond Bial
Map copyright © 2004 by Marshall Cavendish Corporation
Map by Rodica Prato

Library of Congress Cataloging-in-Publication Data
Bial, Raymond.
The Chumash / by Raymond Bial.
p. cm. — (Lifeways)
Summary: Discusses the history, culture, social structure, beliefs, and notable people of the Chumash.
Includes bibliographical references and index.
ISBN 0-7614-1681-1
1. Chumash Indians—History—Juvenile literature. 2. Chumash Indians—Social life and customs—Juvenile literature. [1. Chumash Indians. 2. Indians of North America—California.] I. Title.
II. Series: Bial, Raymond. Lifeways.
E99.C815B53 2003
979.4004'9757—dc21
2003001446

Printed in Italy
6 5 4 3 2 1

Photo Research by Anne Burns Images

Cover Photos by Raymond Bial

All of the photographs in this book are used with permission and through the courtesy of Raymond Bial, with the exception of the following which are used with permission and through the courtesy of: *Santa Barbara Historical Society*: pp. 84, 85, 111, 112; *The Bancroft Library*: pp. 88, 89, 94.

This book is dedicated
to the Chumash who have
long made their home
in the mountains, valleys,
and coastal islands of California.

Contents

Author's Note

At the dawn of the twentieth century, Native Americans were thought to be a vanishing race. However, despite four hundred years of warfare, deprivation, and disease, American Indians have not gone away. Countless thousands have lost their lives, but over the course of this century the populations of native tribes have grown tremendously. Even as American Indians struggle to adapt to modern Western life, they have also kept the flame of their traditions alive—the language, religion, stories, and the everyday ways of life. An exhilarating renaissance in Native American culture is now sweeping the nation from coast to coast.

The Lifeways books depict the social and cultural life of the major nations, from the early history of native peoples in North America to their present-day struggles for survival and dignity. Historical and contemporary photographs of traditional subjects, as well as period illustrations, are blended throughout each book so that readers may gain a sense of family life in a tipi, a hogan, or a longhouse.

No single book can comprehensively portray the intricate and varied lifeways of an entire tribe, or nation. I only hope that young people will come away with a deeper appreciation for the rich tapestry of Indian culture—both then and now—and a keen desire to learn more about these first Americans.

1. Origins

Silhouetted against the setting sun, these mountains of southern California have long been the home of the Chumash.

FOR THOUSANDS OF YEARS, THE CHUMASH (CHOO-MASH) LIVED IN scattered villages along the Pacific Coast, on the Channel Islands, and the mountains of the Coast Ranges of southern California. The Chumash hunted, fished, and gathered to sustain themselves. For generations they held sacred rituals and told stories that helped to define their tribe.

The Chumash believed that there were three worlds: the one on which people lived, the one above it, and one below it. In the lower world lived dangerous and frightening creatures. People inhabited the middle world—a large island surrounded by water. This middle world was held up by two huge serpents. When these serpents became tired and moved, they triggered earthquakes. In the world above, there lived the powerful Sky People who brought good and evil to the middle world.

Here is a story about how the Sky People created the first human beings:

The Making of People

Long ago there was a great flood. After this flood, Coyote and Eagle, who lived in the sky, and Sun, Moon, and Morning Star talked about making the first human beings. Night after night Coyote and Eagle argued whether these people should have hands like Coyote. Lizard only listened. Coyote declared that the people should all be made in his image since he had the finest hands.

At last, Coyote got his way, and everyone agreed that people would have hands like those of Coyote. The next day they gathered around a beautiful white rock in the sky. The rock was symmetrical and flat on top. The rock also had such a fine texture that whatever touched it left an exact impression.

Coyote was just about to place his hand on the rock when Lizard quickly reached out and placed his own hand on the rock. A perfect imprint of Lizard's hand remained on the smooth surface. Enraged, Coyote chased Lizard and tried to kill him, but Lizard escaped by skittering down into a deep ravine.

Eagle and Sun approved of the impression made by Lizard, and Coyote could do nothing to change it. It is said that the impression is still on that rock in the sky, and people now have hands like those of Lizard. If Lizard had not made that print, people would today have paws like those of Coyote.

Early History

The Chumash were not a single tribe or nation. They formed a loosely allied network of seventy-five to one hundred independent villages in southern and central California. The people in these communities spoke six and perhaps as many as eight distinct, yet related, languages. Before the arrival of the Spanish, the Chumash territory encompassed about seven thousand square miles, with villages located in three regions: the Channel Islands, the Pacific Coast, and the interior mountains. The Island Chumash lived on Santa Cruz, Santa Rosa, San Miguel, and Anacapa Islands of the Channel Islands. The Coastal Chumash, which included the Ventureño, Barbareño, Ynezeño, Purisimeño, and the Obispeño, lived along the

Chumash Traditional Homeland

Obispeño

Santa Maria River

Cuyama River

Cuyama

Emigdiano

Castac

Mount Pinos

Purisimeño

Santa Ynez River

Ynezeño

SANTA YNEZ MOUNTAINS

Sespe River

Barbareño

Ventureño

Santa Clara River

Santa Barbara Channel

San Miguel Island

Santa Cruz Island

Anacapa Island

Santa Rosa Island

PACIFIC OCEAN

NEVADA

CALIFORNIA

Chumash homeland

PACIFIC OCEAN

For generations, the Chumash prospered in the mountains, on the Channel Islands, and along the coast of southern California.

coast. The Interior Chumash lived in the mountains. The name "Chumash," now used for all these groups, was originally a Coastal Chumash word that referred only to the Island Chumash living on Santa Rosa Island. The similar name Michumash referred to the people of Santa Cruz Island.

Most of the villages were clustered along 250 miles of the Pacific coast, from San Luis Obispo to Malibu Canyon. The coastal communities were usually situated along the mouths of streams and rivers, which supplied fresh water and a means of travel by canoe. The villages of the Interior Chumash were tucked away among the jagged mountains of present-day Santa Barbara County. They lived as far as seventy-five miles inland, to the western edge of the San Joaquin Valley. The spiritual heart of Chumash territory was Mount Pinos, which towers to nearly 9,000 feet and is northeast of Santa Barbara.

Tracing their ancestry from an ancient people known as Milling Stone Indians, the Chumash have lived in this region of varied terrain and mild weather for more than 10,000 years. Over many generations, they developed one of native California's most complex societies. By the sixteenth century, the scattered villages shared a similar political and social organization and customs. They had also established an extensive trade network. Before the arrival of the Spanish, the population of the Chumash may have been as few as 8,000 or as many as 22,000.

From one generation to the next, the Chumash relied on the land and water to provide them with food, clothing, and shelter. However, from the moment of first contact with Europeans in the sixteenth century, the Chumash way of life began to change dramatically.

The People and the Land

During the Ice Age, when glaciers stored much of the earth's water, the oceans were lower. The Channel Islands were joined to the mainland by a peninsula that extended from the Santa Barbara mainland. Many animals, including mammoths, moved westward onto the peninsula and became isolated when the glaciers melted and the rising ocean again separated the islands from the mainland. As the sea levels remained stable, unique animals evolved on the islands, including a dwarf mammoth (now extinct) and distinct species of fox, skunk, and mice. Unusual plants, such as a rare kind of ironwood, also developed on the islands. The climate was mild for most of the year. However, strong winds, often carrying a veil of misty rain, occasionally swept over the islands, especially during the winter.

The geography of each island was distinct. The westernmost island, San Miguel, was marked by ridges of sandstone and volcanic rock. Two hills rose from the middle of the island, much of which was once blanketed with sumac and manzanita, along with shifting dunes. There were no streams on this island—just one spring near Cuyler Harbor and a few seeps of freshwater in the rocks. East of San Miguel lies the larger island of Santa Rosa. Its rounded hills were carpeted with grass, bushes, and cactus. Canyons held freshwater springs and streams, as well as clusters of oak and pine trees.

Vividly blue in the light of late afternoon, streams and rivers thread their way through the valleys of Chumash territory.

On its small, eastern coast, there were stretches of beach and ranges of low cliffs. East of Santa Rosa was the island of Santa Cruz. The largest of the four islands, Santa Cruz consisted of mountains thrusting upward from the ocean, the tallest of which reached to 2,400 feet. Stands of oak, pine, and island ironwood thrived in the one large valley. There were also deep ravines laced by streams of clear water. The coastline was composed of many high, formidable cliffs, but the island also had a few beaches of cobblestones on

*T*hroughout the course of the seasons, the Chumash hunted and gathered in the deep forests and open valleys near their villages.

which the Chumash were able to land their canoes. Located east of Santa Cruz and just twelve miles from the mainland, Anacapa was the smallest of the islands. It was actually a group of three small islands, all made up of volcanic rock. The Anacapas are in the form of flattopped plateaus and range from ninety to three hundred feet high. Most of the island was bounded by sheer cliffs, but the Chumash gathered abalone from among the shallow rocks on the north shore. They also hunted seals and sea lions that occupied areas of the island. Because there was little freshwater on the island, the Chumash visited Anacapa only seasonally, establishing only fishing camps there.

Most of the Chumash lived along the coast of the mainland directly across the channel from the islands. Here, the waves of the Pacific Ocean lapped the sandy, rock-strewn beaches of a narrow coastal plain. Just beyond the glimmering shoreline, cliffs rose suddenly, like rocky shelves. The cliffs not only offered a breathtaking view of the Pacific Ocean but also hinted at the difficult terrain farther inland. Just beyond the cliffs rose that portion of the southern Coast Ranges known as the Santa Ynez Mountains. Covered with chaparral and dense forests, these mountains reached high into the cloud–dappled sky. Along the coastal plain, the climate remained mild throughout the year and the ocean provided a rich bounty of food. Many Chumash settled here in villages strung along the coast from Ventura to Point Conception. Other groups of Coastal Chumash settled as far north as Estero Bay. Here, the smooth beaches rose to sandy dunes, and then abruptly to rocky terraces and hills, occasionally interrupted by small valleys and streams. Still other coastal groups had their villages east of Ventura and south to Malibu Canyon. Closely related to these coastal dwellers were nearby island groups that had villages along the Santa Ynez and Santa Clara Rivers.

The Interior Chumash lived among the mountains and rivers between the San Joaquin Valley and the Santa Ynez River. They were divided into three groups; the Cuyama, the Emigdiano, and the Castac. Their varied territory included a barren stretch called the Carrizo Plain, lush grasslands dotted with oak trees, and mountains blanketed with thick forests. Here, the Chumash had to deal with very hot summers and chilly winters, yet they had a bounty of food from plants and animals. In the craggy land of peaks and valleys, the Interior Chumash left hundreds of startlingly beautiful and mysterious rock paintings hidden away in caves.

2. Villages

Many Chumash established their villages on the low, flat land overlooking the beaches of the Pacific Ocean.

THE DAILY LIFE OF THE CHUMASH WAS CENTERED IN THE VILLAGE. AT ONE time, there may have been as many as a hundred villages dotting their ancestral territory. Some villages were large enough to be considered towns, while others were composed of only a few dwellings and a handful of people. The largest settlements were situated along the Santa Barbara Channel. These villages served as both capitals and trading centers for the Island and Interior Chumash. Villages were located on high ground near a stream, spring, or other source of freshwater. Ideally, a large village was also near a marsh where the reeds of the bulrush, known as *tule*, could be gathered for use in thatching houses. There also had to be good beaches for landing the numerous canoes.

Each village had traditional rights to certain territories for hunting, fishing, and gathering. Many of these areas were near the community, but, in some cases, people made long, seasonal journeys to places far from their homes. They set up a temporary camp and worked there for a few days or weeks. Then they returned to their village with baskets laden with food.

Two villages might argue about rights to certain lands. Such disputes were usually settled by a ritual battle. To resolve most conflicts, the Chumash engaged in ritual battles in which the opponents lined up facing each other. Taking turns, one man from each side shot an arrow at the opposing side. When one or perhaps several men were killed, the battle was considered over. Leaders often managed to resolve quarrels through negotiations, with no one getting injured or killed. Villagers sometimes had to defend themselves from attack or went to

The Chumash gathered in communities situated between the inland mountains and the sandy beaches, as well as on the coastal islands.

war to drive intruders from their territory. Other times, they avenged insults such as the refusal of a chief to accept an invitation to a feast or dance. However, every military venture was carefully considered beforehand, and the Chumash rarely engaged in actual warfare.

Chumash Houses

Chumash villages generally had between fifteen and fifty bowl-shaped dwellings. The Chumash house, or *'ap*, was built by setting willow poles in the ground in a circle. These supple poles were then bent inward and lashed at the center to form a dome. Smaller saplings or branches were next tied horizontally to form a lattice structure. Then, starting at the bottom, the frame was covered with bundles of tule. Like shingles on a roof, each row of tule formed a layer that overlapped the one below, so that the thatching readily shed the rain. The bundles of tule were tied down so the wind would not blow them away.

There were no windows in the 'ap. Sunlight and fresh air came from the arched doorway and a smoke hole in the top. Sometimes framed by the ribs of a whale, the doorway was covered with a woven tule mat in cold weather or when the owners were away from home. During inclement weather, the smoke hole was covered with a skin to keep out the rain. Women usually cooked outside, but during rainy weather they prepared meals over a fire built in a shallow pit in the center of the house. This fire also provided warmth on chilly nights.

Houses ranged in size from twelve to twenty feet in diameter. A family, including grandparents and sometimes other relatives, lived in

This replica of a home at the Chumash Interpretive Center suggests the size and shape of the traditional family dwelling.

the 'ap. The chief's house was larger—up to thirty-five feet in diameter—to accommodate the many relatives living with him. He was often the only man in the village who had more than one wife. The Interior Chumash typically lived in small, single-family dwellings, while the Coastal Chumash lived in larger houses. A few seaside dwellings may have been as large as fifty feet in diameter. These houses could shelter between forty and seventy people.

Inside the 'ap, tule mats covered the dirt floor. Some houses were furnished with raised, wood-frame platforms covered with tule mats that served as beds. In a few large houses, tule mats were hung like curtains to form sleeping rooms. However, such rooms were not common among California tribes. Household utensils included baskets, hardwood bowls, soapstone pots, and other finely crafted objects.

An underground sweathouse, or 'apa'yik, was located next to most houses. The sweathouse was also known as a *temascal*, a Spanish word derived from the Aztec language. Dug partly underground, the sweathouse was entered through a ladder in a curved roof made of poles and covered with thatch and mud. In some villages, both men and women could enter the sweathouses; in others, only men were allowed inside. Within these sweathouses, the Chumash purified themselves daily with a refreshing sweat bath. Sweathouses were heated by hot stones that had been baked over a fire. The hot rocks were placed in a pit in the middle of the floor. Sometimes, they splashed water over the stones to increase the humidity. The air became very hot as people sat in the dark space. Occasionally they

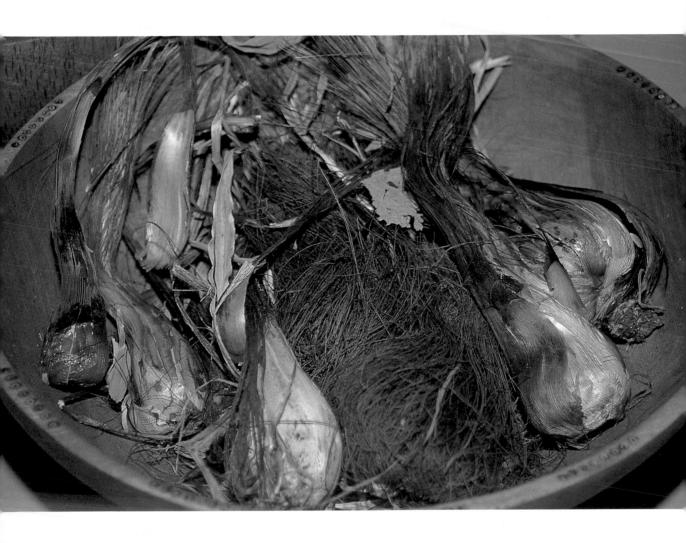

Handmade utensils, such as this hardwood bowl, were common items in a Chumash home.

went outside to plunge into the cold water of the ocean or a nearby creek, after which they returned to the sweathouse. People used sweathouses primarily to cleanse their bodies and spirits. However, if a hunter was preparing to stalk deer and other game, herbs were sometimes burned to mask his scent. Large sweathouses also served as meeting places for the men. Occasionally, women and children used the sweathouses to treat illnesses and participate in ceremonies.

Other village buildings included storehouses which were often placed near the houses. Large amounts of food were kept in a big storehouse near the chief's house. The chief needed a generous supply of food because he often had to entertain people and provide for the needy. Each village also had a smooth, level field where contests, such as shinny, kick ball, and hoop-and-pole, and ball games played against other villages were held. The field was often surrounded by a low wall.

A village also had a dance ground for religious ceremonies. Within the dance ground was the *siliyik*. The siliyik consisted of a semicircular area enclosed by a high fence of tule mats. Here priests and shamans conducted rituals. Outside the siliyik, people sat around campfires where they were sheltered by a tule-mat windbreak.

At work areas people chipped stone tools and weapons, built canoes, wove baskets, and pounded acorns. There was also a cemetery for burials.

The houses and other structures were loosely situated along a main street. In larger villages, houses were arranged in rows, with paths running like streets between them. Paths led from one house to another, as well as to the common areas. The Chumash lives were centered around family, friends, and work. They lived peacefully and labored hard to provide for themselves, practice their religion, and enjoy games and stories.

Social Organization

The Chumash did not have a single ruler for the entire people. Each village was led by a chief called a *wot* (rhymes with "boat"). The wot inherited his position from his father and other male ancestors, or he became the leader due to his wealth and influence. Occasionally, women became wots. Some communities had more than one chief, who were most likely the heads of prominent families. Larger villages, such as Syukhtun, which was located at the site of Santa Barbara, and Shisholop, which was situated at the present-day city of Ventura, usually had three or four leaders, one of whom served as head chief. The wots granted hunting and fishing rights, managed hunting and gathering activities, oversaw religious ceremonies, and in rare instances, led the men of the village into battle. Wots made sure that enough food was set aside for religious and social celebrations. Among their most important duties was to ensure the care of the poor and the elderly in the community.

Some areas of Chumash territory were politically organized into an alliance of several villages. The village leaders then formed a regional council and one was selected as *paqwot*, or head chief. The head chief's assistant, known as the *paha*, managed major religious ceremonies, such as the acorn harvest festival in the autumn and the Winter Solstice Ceremony.

The Chumash community was further organized into three social classes: artisans, shamans, and relatives of the wot. The artisans formed guilds to carry on their various trades. Shamans, who were responsible for the spiritual and physical welfare of the people, cured illnesses and injuries, interpreted dreams, and guided vision quests. The third class was composed of the people who were related to the wot. Other notable people were special messengers of the leaders known as the *ksen*. The messengers traveled from village to village, making announcements and gathering news.

Another key group was the prestigious *'antap* society. Members of this secret society sang and danced at ceremonies and served as advisors to the wot. Only people from upper-class families could join this secret society, which included the wot, members of the wot's family, shamans, the village paha, and other officials. The 'antap held special ceremonies to ensure a balance in the universe. It arranged the key activities, such as the gathering, storage, and distribution of food, that ensured the well-being of the community. The 'antap also forecast weather, named children, and determined the dates and locations of important ceremonies.

Chumash society was organized into clans named for animals such as the bear, eagle, or coyote. Clan members considered themselves to be related to a common ancestor. Each clan was responsible for certain duties relating to government, sustenance, and rituals. For example, like the eagle, the leader of the animals, members of the Eagle clan were most likely to be wots. Clans were also ranked according to their prestige. The Eagle, Bear, and Snow Goose Clans were more highly regarded than the Coyote, Raven, and Dog Clans. Children were born into their mother's clan. Members of different clans lived in the same village, but loyalty to the village was more important than clan membership. People painted their bodies with distinct styles to indicate the village where they lived.

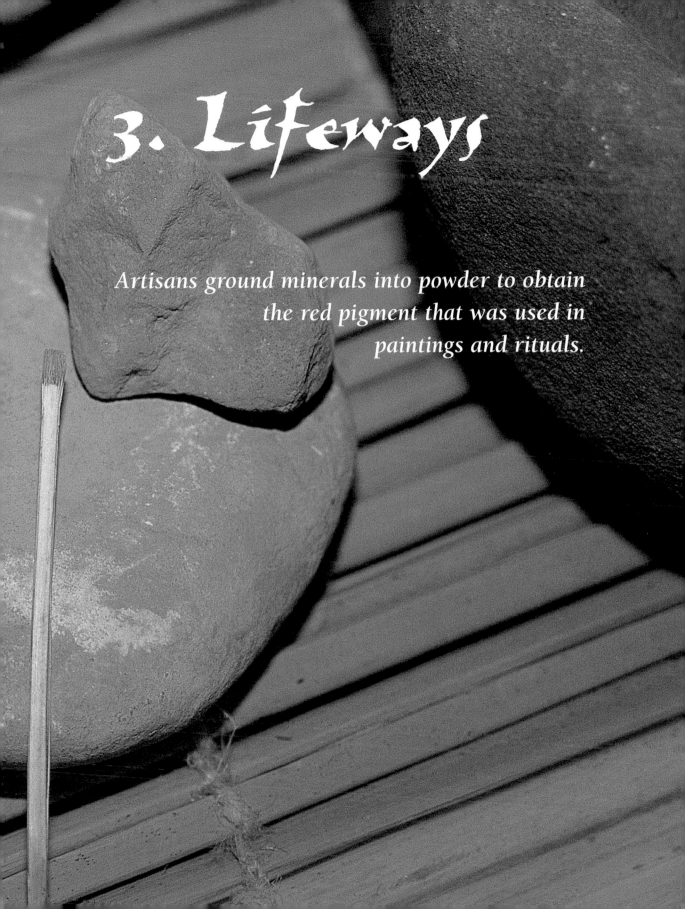

3. Lifeways

Artisans ground minerals into powder to obtain the red pigment that was used in paintings and rituals.

Cycle of Life

The survival of the Chumash depended on families working every day to provide themselves with food, clothing, and shelter. The men ventured from their villages to hunt game in the mountains or to catch fish in the sea. Women and children dug roots and picked berries in the meadows and the forests. During the cycle of days and seasons, individuals, families, and villagers also experienced the key events of life—birth, childhood, coming-of-age, marriage, and death. For each occasion, they followed time-honored customs and rituals.

Birth. The Chumash loved their children and looked forward to the birth of a new baby. When a woman was about to give birth, she made a hole in the ground wherever she happened to be at that time. The hole was warmed by a fire and then lined with clean straw. Here, she delivered her baby, often with the assistance of an older woman. After giving birth, the mother bathed herself in cold water.

Childhood. The Chumash were gentle people who were rarely angry with their children. Encouraged to behave themselves, children were seldom punished. As they grew up, boys and girls learned their roles in the village and the skills they would need to survive as adults. Girls learned to gather food, cook meals, care for children, and manage the household. Their mother and other women instructed them in handicrafts, such as basket making.

As they grew up, children learned many important skills, including the crafting of sharp points for arrows and spears.

Boys learned to hunt and fish and to defend themselves against enemies. They learned various crafts, such as how to make tools and weapons, and were also taught the important roles of governing the village and participating in religious ceremonies.

Coming-of-Age. When a young woman had her first period, she was no longer allowed to eat certain foods, such as meat and grease. She also could not gaze into a fire. As boys and girls approached adulthood, they were taken out at night and given a strong drink made from pounded *toloache* root mixed with water. This intoxicating beverage induced visions in which it was believed the youth saw their futures.

Once they had undertaken these rituals and learned to provide for themselves, young women and men were then considered ready to be married.

Marriage. Men and women from the same village sometimes married each other. However, people more often chose spouses from other villages. These marriages served to strengthen the bonds among the various communities. People also did not marry within their clan. The men usually offered gifts, such as beads, otter skins, or blankets, to the parents in exchange for permission to marry their daughter. The wedding ceremony often included a lively dance by a man known as "the jealous one." With a pair of pelican wings tied to his head and a bow in his hand, he danced with a woman in a feather cape while another man sang about the wedding night. After a couple was married, they usually lived with the wife's relatives in her village. Only the chief and a few wealthy men could afford more than one wife. Adultery was strictly forbidden and was punished by whipping. Couples generally remained devoted to each other for their entire lives.

Death. People mourned the death of loved ones in elaborate funeral ceremonies. The body was carried to a sacred place where a ceremony was held around a large fire. Mourners watched over the body. Then, led by a shaman smoking a pipe, they sang and passed by the body three times. Each time, the mourners lifted the animal skin covering the body and the shaman blew three mouthfuls of smoke over the body. The relatives of the deceased offered beads to the chief, and then the mourners cried out in grief as they proceeded with the body to a cemetery enclosed by a high stockade.

The body was usually buried facedown; only the Island Chumash buried their dead faceup. The body was laid in a flexed position, with the head to the west. Offerings such as beads, bowls, and weapons were often included in the burial. The cemetery was regarded as sacred ground. Graves were marked with a wooden plank, often painted with black-and-white squares. Sometimes, a pole was raised over the grave from which important objects from the deceased's life were hung. These might include the hooks and line of a fisherman or the bows and arrows of a hunter. Sometimes, personal belongings of the deceased or a whale rib, bent like a bow, were laid over the grave.

Hunting and Gathering

Unlike some native people, the Chumash did not plant corn or other crops. The Pacific Coast and islands abounded in sources of food. From the sea, they caught over a hundred kinds of fish. They occasionally had to camp while they hunted, fished, or collected plants, but they never had to travel far from their villages to find food. Their settled way of life allowed them more time to

pursue artistic endeavors. However, the Chumash who lived in the mountains faced greater challenges in dealing with the rough terrain and finding game. Each family was responsible for providing for its own members—women gathered while men hunted. However, in some large villages, individuals who became skilled at fishing or handicrafts such as basket making worked in exchange for material objects and food.

The Chumash who lived inland hunted for game in the rocky hills and valleys around their villages.

The Chumash originally used a throwing spear known as an *atlatl* to hunt elk, deer, and sea mammals. Beginning about 1,500 years ago, they began to use bows and arrows. To catch fish on the open sea and from along the rivers, they used a variety of methods, including dip nets, traps, and baskets. They caught small fish with fishhooks made

By lashing together straight, slender branches, men fashioned simple, yet effective box traps for catching small game.

from abalone and mussel shells. They killed larger fish, seals, sea otters, and porpoises with sharp harpoons. They also used the juice of certain plants to poison the water and stun the fish. Along the shore, they gathered clams, mussels, and abalone. They caught crabs in the coastal waters and crayfish in the creeks. Farther inland, men used bows and arrows to hunt mule deer and elk. They used snares and

*W*orking together, women gathered many kinds of wild fruits, berries, nuts, and seeds to help sustain their families.

deadfalls to catch rabbits and other small game. They hunted ducks and geese that touched down in the marshes and lakes.

The Chumash ate food from many kinds of wild plants. They harvested berries, nuts, and seeds, most notably acorns from live oak and valley oak trees, the most important food of the Chumash and other native peoples of California. People also gathered piñon nuts, cherries, and many kinds of roots and bulbs. Foods were prepared and eaten in various ways. Piñon nuts and wild strawberries were eaten raw, while chia seeds were ground into flour. Nuts from the California laurel were roasted and then eaten. Other seeds were toasted and ground to a paste. The Chumash harvested miner's lettuce to use as salad greens. Along the coast, people gathered seaweed which they chopped and dried in an oven or ate raw or boiled. They ate rose hips fresh from the plant or brewed into tea. The tart, sticky berries of the manzanita shrub were made into cider or preserved as a jelly.

The Chumash roasted meat and fish over an open fire and cooked shellfish in soups and stews. Acorns required long and laborious preparation. The dried acorns were first shelled and ground to a powder between two stones called a mortar and pestle. Acorns have bitter tannic acid, which had to be thoroughly leached, or washed away, from the flour. The acorn flour was then mixed with water in a tightly woven basket and cooked with heated stones placed in the liquid. Women stirred the mixture as it came to a boil and gradually thickened into a mush. The Chumash enjoyed this thick acorn soup along with fish and meat at every meal.

Acorn Bread

Ingredients

1 cup acorn flour
1/2 cup cornmeal
1/2 cup wheat flour
1 tablespoon baking soda
1 teaspoon salt

1 cup milk
1 egg, lightly beaten
3 tablespoons vegetable oil
1/4 cup honey

Directions

Carefully crack and shell dry acorns.

Grind the dry, raw acorns into fine flour with a food processor. Place one cup of acorn flour in a colander or strainer lined with muslin or coffee filter paper. Put the colander in a sink and run water through the flour to remove all the bitter taste.

Combine acorn flour with cornmeal, wheat flour, baking soda, and salt. Add milk, egg, honey, and vegetable oil and mix into a moist batter. Pour the batter into a greased pan about eight inches square and bake at 350 degrees for twenty to thirty minutes.

Makes one eight-inch loaf.

Note: Acorn flour may be dried and stored in sealed plastic bags in a freezer. Acorn flour may also be used in place of regular flour in cookie and pancake recipes.

Travel and Trade

The most striking achievement of the Chumash was their distinctive type of boat, which was called a *tomol*. Sturdy and swift, gracefully shaped tomols were used for ocean fishing, for hunting seals, sea lions, and sea otters, and for traveling between the coastal towns. These boats were also crucial to trade between the islands and mainland. In the words of one Chumash man, Fernando Librado, "The canoe was the 'house of the sea.'" A tomol was worth more than a house and only a wealthy person could afford to own one. Every prosperous coastal town had several tomols nosed up onto the beach.

Men built tomols with tools made from animal bones, stones, or shells. They worked patiently, taking at least forty days and often from two to six months to complete a tomol. With whale bone or antler wedges, they split logs into rough boards about three quarters of an inch thick. They preferred redwood, which swelled when wet to seal the cracks between boards. Redwood does not grow near the beaches, but redwood logs floated as driftwood from the forests of northern California where the trees grew in abundance along the coast. They also used pine and sometimes other driftwood. With shell and stone tools, they scraped the surface of the planks. Starting with a heavy plank for the bottom, they glued three or four rows of planks together, edge to edge, with *yop*, a mixture of hot pitch and asphalt, a kind of tar that washed onto the beaches. These planks formed each side of the tomol. After the yop had dried, holes were drilled in the planks and the planks were lashed together with twine made from milkweed plants. The holes and seams were sealed with more yop. The surface of the canoe was then smoothed with sandstone and lightly sanded with sharkskin. The craftsmen coated the tomol with a mixture of tar, pine pitch, and red paint to make sure the vessel was completely waterproof. Along with the red paint, the tomol was often decorated with abalone shells. Craftsmen also made two or three long paddles, shaped like a shovel at each end.

Ranging in length from twelve to thirty feet, a tomol could carry a crew of three or four and a considerable amount of goods. Large canoes could transport twelve people and some as many as twenty people. When finished, the tomol was carried to the edge of the water. The builders offered a prayer and then dragged the canoe through the surf. It was loaded with goods and people, with the captain in the stern, or back. One crew member, usually a young boy or an old man, sat in the middle of the canoe and with a basket or abalone shell bailed water that seeped into the tomol. Quite seaworthy, tomols were known to have been navigated with double-bladed paddles as far as sixty-five miles into the open ocean.

A highly regarded group of men, known as the Brotherhood of the Tomol, knew how to make these distinctive canoes and paddle them across the Santa Barbara Channel. If a young man wanted to learn how to make a tomol, he had to ask if he could join the brotherhood. If approved, he paid a fee and was then accepted as a brother and taught the secrets of the craft. Members of the brotherhood also knew how to ferry island goods, such as stone blades

*T*he Chumash crafted long, gracefully shaped canoes that they used for fishing and traveling between the islands and the mainland.

and drills, and fish, such as shark, bonito, and halibut, to the mainland. Every brother helped a brother in times of trouble. Brothers became rich and respected since they could travel far out to sea and catch the largest fish. They could also journey great distances and bring back impressive quantities of food, tools, and ornaments. They even traveled as far as Santa Catalina Island where they traded for highly prized soapstone bowls.

No one is sure how long tomols lasted—it depended on how often they were used and how well they were maintained. The Chumash usually stored their tomols in a moist, shady area until they were needed for a sea journey. Before embarking, they inspected the vessel carefully and made any necessary repairs. If they took good care of their tomol, it would remain seaworthy for many years. Around 1850, the Chumash made the last tomols to be used for fishing and trade expeditions. In 1913, an elderly Chumash man, Fernando Librado, constructed a tomol for anthropologist John P. Harrington, to demonstrate how the canoes were built. When he was a young man, Librado had observed the last tomols being built by older men in his village. Since the 1970s, a number of tomols have been made.

The Chumash were great traders who exchanged a wide variety of goods among themselves and with other native peoples. They often bartered for goods or used strings of shell beads as money to purchase items. Among the native peoples of California, the Chumash were the primary source for the shells that were used as money. This money, called 'anchum, was made from various clams and snail shells but most

*T*he Chumash carved many small objects, including beads used as a kind of money known as 'anchum.

often from the olivella. This shell comes from a marine snail. People living on the Channel Islands, especially those on Santa Cruz Island, specialized in making the bead money. They served as the mint, or source of currency, for the Chumash living on the mainland. It is believed that the words *Chumash* and *'anchum* are related and that the name *Chumash* once had something to do with the making of bead money by the Island Chumash. The value of the money depended on the rarity of the shell and the difficulty of manufacture. Beads made from the callus, the thick part of the shell near the opening, were worth twice as much as beads made from the wall of the shell, because fewer beads could be made from the smaller callus. People determined the value of the beads by the rarity of the shell and the length of the strand—according to the number of times it could be wrapped around one's hand. Eight strings of beads are thought to have equaled one Spanish silver dollar.

Deer and rabbits did not live on the islands. So, the Island Chumash paddled to the mainland where they used shell beads to buy rabbit skins, deerskins, and antlers. They also traded their fish, fish oils, sea lion meat, sea otter pelts, whale bones, and other ocean bounty for foods that were scarce on the islands, such as acorns, pine nuts, chia seeds, and wild cherries. The Chumash who lived in the interior valleys journeyed on foot to the coast and traded for shells and beads, asphalt, fish, sea otter pelts, and other goods that they needed. In exchange, Inland Chumash offered black pigment, obsidian, antelope and elk skins, nuts, seeds, and herbs.

The trade network extended beyond the Chumash to other tribes in the region. Black steatite, or soapstone, dug from Santa Catalina Island—to the south of Chumash territory—was taken eastward as far as the Colorado River and traded to Yuman peoples. The Chumash word for Santa Catalina Island was *huya*, meaning steatite. Steatite, or soapstone, was valued because it could be carved as easily as soap into pipes, sacred figures, and beads. Large chunks of soapstone were also carved into bowls, which, unlike sandstone bowls, did not break when heated over a fire. The Chumash traded with the Yokut in the Sierra Nevada for obsidian, a glasslike volcanic rock that made excellent arrowheads and knife blades. The Yokut also offered exotic goods, such as pouches of tobacco and sweet cakes of honeydew gathered from plants. The Chumash also bartered with the Mohave who lived on the Colorado River, near the present-day California-Arizona border. The Mohave journeyed across deserts and mountains for as long as two weeks to offer the Chumash highly sought-after goods, including pottery, cotton blankets, and the mineral known as hematite, or red ocher. The Chumash used this red mineral for body painting, cave painting, and canoe decorations.

Because they traded in so many valuable goods, the Chumash prospered. They enjoyed a variety of food obtained through barter. They were able to fashion excellent tools and weapons and make jewelry from materials obtained through trade. They wore paths deep in the hillsides and along the canyons. When the Spanish arrived in the 1760s, they rode the same trails on horseback. Years

Pigments were used to decorate utensils, such as handcrafted baskets, and to create rock paintings.

later, from the early 1800s well into the 1900s, the trails became the paved roads and railroad routes of the region. Today, other rugged paths have been preserved as hiking trails and country roads, such as Refugio Pass Road. This road once connected the villages of Santa Ynez with the coastal town of Qasil, which was located at present-day Refugio Beach. At one time, Qasil was a hub where the Coastal and Island Chumash came together to trade and hold ceremonies.

Clothing and Jewelry

In the mild climate of southern California, the Chumash wore little or no clothing. Men often wore nothing except a belt or a small net around their waists from which they hung tools. If the weather turned chilly, they might wrap an animal skin around their waist. Women typically wore a skirt formed by two aprons— a wide one in back and a narrow one in front. The knee-length aprons were made of buckskin, shredded bark, or grass fringed

*W*omen sewed soft, yet durable buckskin into comfortable garments and adorned them with beads or shells.

*B*oth men and women wore jewelry like this necklace strung with beads and acorns.

with abalone shells. People usually went barefoot, but occasionally they wore a type of socks fashioned from deerskin. When men went to war they wore sandals made of plant fibers. As winter set in, people wrapped themselves in capes of animal skins. The poor could only afford clothing made of grasses and shredded bark. Prosperous Chumash put on cloaks of bear and other furs. An ankle-length fur cloak indicated a man's high status in the village. A chief often wore a waist-length bearskin cape as a sign of his prominent social position.

Both men and women tied up their long hair with the strings woven through it. People wore shell, bone, and stone necklaces. Men occasionally pierced their noses. Many pierced their ears, making large holes from which they hung pouches for their tobacco. They often painted their bodies, and for special ceremonies, they wore more body paint and jewelry. Ceremonial dancers and singers wore feathered skirts, headdresses, and other elaborate regalia depicting animals or birds. This attire might be made from bearskins, twisted milkweed fiber, or feathers from the California condor.

Handicrafts

The Chumash were highly regarded craftspeople. The tomol is perhaps the best example of their great skill and artistry. However, they made many other objects. They expertly carved wooden plates, bowls, trays, and boxes. They also used wood for harpoon shafts and other hunting and fishing equipment. The Chumash preferred chert, a kind of flint, and occasionally obsidian for making points for arrows and spears. They also chipped pieces of flint into knives, scrapers, drills, and other tools. They fashioned many other tools and cooking utensils from stone and especially from soapstone, which they carved into bowls, smoking pipes, and arrow-shaft straighteners. They also made beads, ornaments, and animal figures that served as charms. Serpentine, another soft stone, was made into doughnut shapes that were fitted over digging sticks to provide added weight. Sandstone was shaped into bowls used for grinding seeds.

Artisans carved wood and bone into flutes, whistles, and rattles. Bone was also used to make fishhooks, needles, awls, and hairpins. It was made into wedges and gouges for woodworking and into flakers for chipping arrowheads. People who lived along the ocean made stools from the vertebrae of whales. The Chumash fashioned shells, including abalone, clam, and olivella shells, into beads, ornaments, and money. Plant fibers were made into houses and clothing. Yucca fibers were made into thick cords for harpoon lines. Fibers of hemp, nettle, and milkweed were twisted into string. The Chumash wove this string into fishnets and bags.

The Chumash are celebrated for their finely woven, carefully decorated baskets. These were needed in almost every area of daily life. Some baskets were made as gifts; others were used in grinding seeds and nuts. Many served as storage containers. Even water was stored in large baskets. Sealed on the inside with asphalt, these baskets could hold up to six gallons of water. People used baskets for gathering, storing, preparing, and serving foods. They kept their money and other valuables in baskets, and measured acorns for trade in baskets. They toted babies

Chumash men chipped flint into sharp arrow points, that they then tied to the tips of wooden shafts with thin, tough sinew.

Chumash women made baskets in many shapes and sizes, useful for gathering, storing, and preparing foods.

History. Fortunately, contemporary weavers have carefully studied many of these baskets and John P. Harrington's early interviews with basket makers. They have learned to work with the wild plant materials and to again make traditional Chumash baskets. These baskets are a source of inspiration for a new generation of Chumash weavers whose dedication ensures that this art form will flourish well into the future.

4. Beliefs

The universe of the Chumash was made up of
three layers—the earth, the world below,
and the world above.

IN THEIR TRADITIONAL RELIGION, THE CHUMASH BELIEVED THAT THE universe was composed of three worlds layered upon each other like flat, circular trays. The middle world was the earth, or the "World of the People." In the world above lived powerful beings, including the Sun, Moon, Morning Star, and the other Sky People. The lower world was inhabited by dangerous creatures, known as *nunashish*, who rose to the middle world at night and frightened anyone who encountered them.

The Chumash believed that long ago, before there were humans, an earlier people known as the First People inhabited the middle world. These First People lived much like the Chumash, but there was a great flood and most of the First People were turned into animals, plants, and natural forces, such as thunder. Some of the First People escaped by ascending into the sky where they became the Sky People. A council of the Sky People led to the creation of humans, and the Sky People were revered as the most powerful beings in the universe. Like humans, they had intelligence and emotion, and they often acted unpredictably to bring good or evil. For example, Sun brought warmth, but could also make the earth too hot or seemingly vanish so that cold weather swept over the land. The Chumash were so fascinated by the night sky that shamans also served as astronomers who could explain the workings of the universe to their people. The Chumash likely saw a relationship between the afterlife and the universe. In one story, a dead woman encountered many obstacles as she journeyed along a path through the Milky Way.

The Chumash believed that powerful spiritual beings known as the Sky People lived in the world above.

The Chumash also believed that all human and supernatural beings sought to gain more power over good and evil. To do so, the person practiced secret rituals through which he called upon a dream helper. The helper could be an animal, plant, insect, distant star, planet, or a natural force such as thunder. Among the most important helpers were Bear, Eagle, Beaver, Thunder, and Whirlwind. Dream helpers could be called upon to assist with basket making, a long canoe journey, or gambling, or in times of peril from enemy attack or natural disaster.

To acquire a dream helper, one went on a vision quest. With the aid of a shaman, the seeker fasted and drank toloache, a hallucinogenic beverage made from pounded roots. This dangerous drink was consumed in the belief that it allowed an individual to directly appeal to a dream helper. If a dream helper appeared in the vision, the seeker then made a talisman known as an *'atishwin* that represented the helper. Thereafter, the talisman was carefully protected. Misfortune befell the person who allowed the 'atishwin to be lost or stolen. Shamans, chiefs, and other prominent individuals often had more than one dream helper, an indication of their great power in the village. By contrast, those who had no dream helper were regarded as frightened, helpless, and easily dominated by more powerful individuals.

Spiritual guidance was provided by the shamans. It was believed that shamans received their power from a spirit who appeared to them in a vision. Wearing bearskin garments and belts hung with deer hooves, shamans acted as doctors who believed that sickness was caused by a patient's spiritual problems. They cured injuries and illness with ritual songs, dances, and prayers, herbal medicines, and polished stone charms. Shamans also used a hollow tube for blowing away or sucking out a patient's evil spirits. The patient was cured once an object was supposedly removed from the body, although the object was a stone or small animal that the shaman had actually brought with him.

To treat various maladies, the Chumash used nearly a hundred medicines obtained from the bark, roots, and flowers of various plants. Nettle was used to ease rheumatism and paralysis. The shaman made a bed of cut stalks on which the patient would lay and vigorously roll around. Or the shaman beat the patient with a

The Chumash treated illnesses with medicines made from the bark, roots, and flowers of a variety of plants.

handful of nettle stalks. The Chumash used willow bark for sore throats and elder flowers for colds. Poison oak was even used to dress wounds. One of their favorite medicines was chuchupate, a root of a plant in the carrot family that grew high in the mountains. People chewed chuchupate to give themselves strength and to ward off illness. They also mixed animal fat with ground minerals and painted it on the patient. Seawater was sometimes drunk to cleanse the digestive system. Another treatment required the patient to swallow live red ants.

Rites and Ceremonies

The Chumash frequently held sacred rituals in their villages at which they danced and sang. They held a mourning ceremony when a person died and gathered to celebrate weddings and induct a new chief. At times, people from several villages came together for a major ceremony. The two most significant ceremonies honored Earth and Sun.

A thanksgiving festival, the Hutash Ceremony, honored the earth goddess, known as Shup or Hutash. She provided the Chumash with food. It was held in late summer or early autumn after the acorn harvest and in major communities such as Muwu, Shisholop, and Syukhtun. People came from miles away, including the Channel Islands, for this large gathering that lasted for five or six days. Spectators sat on tule mats around a sacred area where performers sang and danced. Visiting chiefs sat in special locations marked by painted poles. In the siliyik, unseen by others, two old men blew ceremonial whistles.

Sacred rites followed the cycle of the seasons. The important Winter Solstice Ceremony was held on the shortest day of the year.

On December 21—the shortest day of the year—the Chumash attended the Winter Solstice Ceremony to honor the Sun. On the first day, all debts from the last year had to be settled. The next day, the paha, who was regarded as the image of the Sun and twelve assistants, who were considered rays of the Sun, set up a pole called the Sunstick. About sixteen inches long, the Sunstick had a stone disk on top. This disk was painted with twelve sun rays. These rays were aligned with the sun to cast a circular shadow. With the powerful Sunstick, the paha symbolically drew the Sun back toward the earth to ensure the cycle of the seasons and the growth of plants in the ensuing year.

In all of their ceremonies, the Chumash participated in dances, many of which were social while others were deeply religious. Both men and women danced to the music of flutes, whistles, and occasionally the scattering of seeds. Many dances honored land animals, including the California condor, bear, beaver, fox, coyote, and blackbird. There were also dances for ocean creatures, such as the killer whale, swordfish, and barracuda, and even a seaweed dance. The dancers wore elaborate regalia in which they represented the animal or plant. The performers also adorned themselves with body paint for each of the dances.

The Swordfish Dance was one of the most important rituals. The dancer wore either a swordfish skull inlaid with pieces of shell or a headdress that represented the fish's sword. Offerings of beads and other gifts were made to the swordfish, believed to be the chief of all the sea animals.

The Chumash enjoyed many kinds of songs, including lullabies, gambling songs, songs of joy, storytelling songs, and songs for curing the sick. Songs were part of the ceremonial dances, and were often accompanied by musical instruments. The most important musical instrument was the *wansak'*, or clapper stick, which was made from a partially split elderberry stick. This wooden instrument was played by striking it against the hand to make a clapping sound or by shaking it to make a quick, rattling noise. The clapper stick was used to keep the beat or rhythm of a song or dance. Other popular musical instruments included deer-bone flutes, bird-bone whistles, and rattles made from turtle shells with small pebbles inside.

Rock Painting

The Chumash created strikingly beautiful, yet mysterious rock paintings, or pictographs, in hundreds of caves throughout their homeland. Although these rock paintings were often exquisite, they were not made as art. Hidden away in secret places, they were not intended for public viewing. It is believed that they were made during toloache rites. Shamans most likely painted the cryptic symbols as a means of asking spiritual powers for help in the daily lives of the Chumash. The colorful and complex paintings depicted a variety of figures, including abstract beings resembling birds and fish. Others featured stars and planets, mythic figures, natural forces, and abstract designs. Many of the symbols represented fertility, water, and rain. The circle and a curved line split on the ends were two of the common themes in many paintings.

The pigments for making the paints came from different kinds of minerals. By crushing colored rocks into a fine powder, artists obtained red, blue, yellow, green, brown, gray, and white pigments. Red was obtained from hematite. White came from gypsum

*T*his modern painting of a lizard recalls the long and revered tradition of rock painting among the early Chumash.

or a very fine powder called diatomaceous earth. Black was derived from charcoal or manganese oxide. These minerals were ground and mixed with a liquid binder, usually water, animal fat, or milkweed sap. The Chumash applied this heavy paint with brushes of soap plant, yucca, or animal tails. Sometimes, they painted with their fingers. Dry lumps of pigment were also used like chalk to draw lines.

The majority of the paintings were made on sandstone in rock shelters and caves in valleys and canyons. Paintings with the most

The mysterious, abstract designs of Chumash rock paintings often depicted the planets and the stars, as well as the wind and the rain.

varied and enigmatic symbols were usually created in remote caves. Most of the paintings were made in the mountains. Many rock paintings are believed to be less than one thousand years old, and some are fairly recent. At Painted Cave, for example, complex designs have been painted at various times, often over earlier paintings. It is believed that one painting depicts a solar eclipse that occurred on November 24, 1677. Other figures were made before and after that event, in styles that changed over time.

Rock paintings are held sacred by Chumash today, and the locations of many are kept secret.

Games and Gambling

The Chumash enjoyed competitive games, and they usually gambled on the outcome. They did not believe in luck, but thought that winning or losing the wager was influenced by supernatural powers. Every village had an area, known as a *malamtepupi*, that was set aside for games. The smooth, level ground was sometimes bordered by a low wall. People played other games, such as dice with walnut shells or sticks. Children enjoyed bear tag in which everyone ran from the "bear" who was "it." Boys and young men liked to play hoop-and-pole, or *payas*, with a hoop made from a willow stem wrapped in buckskin. Four or five inches in diameter, the hoop was rolled along the ground in a straight line. Standing to one side about twelve feet away, a contestant waited. As the hoop rolled by he threw a six-foot-long wooden pole like a spear. If he speared the hoop, he scored one point. Sometimes, players shot an arrow at the hoop. Two or more players could compete in this game. The first player to score twelve points won the game.

The Chumash also played the hand game *'alewsa*, with two teams of two or more players on each side. The players of one team had two sticks or bones—one black and one white. They all hid the sticks in their hands, which they held in front of themselves. The object of the game was for the opponents to guess which player held the white stick. The opposing team had a "killer" who made the guess for his team. If he guessed correctly, his team received a counter stick. His team then hid the painted sticks. The

Among the favorite games of boys and young men was payas, a game played with a handcrafted hoop and pole.

game was played until all the counter sticks, as many as fifteen, were won by one side. The hand game is still popular among the Chumash and other native people in California.

One of the most popular team sports among the Chumash was shinny, or *tikauwich*. During major ceremonies, nearly everyone in two competing villages might play against each other, with as many as two or three hundred contestants on the field. The

square field could be as long as three hundred yards on each side and had goalposts at opposite ends. The players carried shinny sticks, which resembled hockey sticks. The object of the game was to hit the small wooden ball through the opponent's goalpost. These games were hotly contested. Women rarely got into fights, but the men frequently brawled. The Ventureño Chumash were reputed to be the best shinny players. It was customary for the

Many people enjoyed the game of shinny, or tikauwich, played with a ball and a shinny stick resembling a hockey stick.

winning team to give half of its winnings in bets to the chief of the village hosting the celebration. This contribution helped to pay for the costs of the event.

Storytelling

Among the Chumash, stories were passed down from one generation to the next. In the evenings, children gathered around the fire to listen to one of their elders. They not only enjoyed these stories, but also learned about their history and traditions through them. Some stories were humorous while others explained the mysteries of the universe, the land, the waters, and the night sky. Stories, such as "The Sky People," described the actions of Coyote and other supernatural beings.

The Sky People

There is a place above where Sun, Morning Star, Coyote, and Eagle play the gambling game peon. There are two players on each side and Moon is the referee. They gather in a special house where only peon can be played. They play every night for a year, staying up until dawn. Coyote likes to bet on the outcome.

On Christmas Eve they count the counter sticks to determine which side won. If Eagle's side comes out ahead, there will be a rainy year. Sun wagers many kinds of food—acorns, deer, wild cherries, seeds, ducks, and geese. If Sun loses, Coyote can hardly wait to receive his payment. He

Chumash stories recounted the activities of the Sky People and the other supernatural beings.

pulls open the door and all his winnings fall to the earth, so that that year people will have plenty of food.

However, if Sun wins Coyote pays him with human lives. Coyote always wants to give old people to him, and Sun squabbles with him. Occasionally, Sun wins the argument and gets to choose a young person to die.

Every day, the Sky People have a particular task. Morning Star shines at dawn, Sun lights the day, and Moon illuminates the night. Moon is a single woman with a house near Sun's house. Moon and Sun never age: they are always there.

Coyote is a powerful and generous spirit, and people have great faith in him. From high in the sky, he watches over the Chumash and provides food for them. Like Sun, Eagle is believed to devour people. He lives in a place surrounded by hills of white bones from the people he has eaten. Eagle has no wife or children. He is always in the sky, where he is always thinking.

The uncle of people, Sun is an old man. He is naked, except for a feather headdress. He carries a torch in his hand that he gradually raises to generate the heat of the day. All day long he follows a trail around the world. During this journey, he rests three times and when he reaches the west in the evening, he quickly returns home, going around to the south.

A widower, Sun lives with his pets and his two unmarried daughters in a large crystal house. His daughters have aprons woven of live rattlesnakes. The house is filled with many kinds of animals—bears, lions, elk, deer, wolves, rattlesnakes, and birds—all of which are tame.

When Sun comes home in the evening, he brings whatever people he has decided to bring with him. If they are large, he tucks them under his belt. If they are babies, he slips them under the band of his headdress. He arrives home in time for supper, and when he first enters there is a dense fog. He throws the people down and as the fog clears he and his daughters cook them with his torch. Sun and his daughters then eat the people. Every day Sun carries off people from the world in this manner.

5. Changing World

Their way of life changed drastically when the Chumash were converted to Christianity and forced to live near Spanish missions.

IN 1542, THE CHUMASH FIRST CAME INTO CONTACT WITH EUROPEANS when the Portuguese commander Juan Rodríguez Cabrillo guided a fleet of Spanish ships along the California coast. He may have been searching for a sea route to China, but was greeted by the Chumash. The friendly Chumash, who were the first California natives to encounter Europeans, paddled out to the ships in boats laden with gifts. Despite the hospitality, Cabrillo claimed all the lands of the Chumash for Spain. In 1602, Spanish explorer Sebastián Vizcaíno sailed into the bay that he named Santa Barbara in honor of the saint's day. Chumash relations with the newcomers remained friendly, even when the Spanish began to use the Santa Barbara Channel as a stopover on voyages across the Pacific Ocean. The Spanish had not yet established a settlement there, and the Chumash continued to thrive for the next 160 years with little direct intrusion from the Europeans.

Europeans did not drastically influence the Chumash way of life until the 1770s, when the Spanish began to build missions and forts known as presidios in their territory. The Spanish, who had established an empire in Mexico and South America, believed that they had to protect California from the Russians and the English who were exploring and trading along the northwest coast. In 1769, Gaspar de Portolá led an expedition to establish missions and presidios in California. In a joint military and religious effort, the soldiers were to protect the settlements while Franciscan priests, known as padres in Spanish, pacified and converted the Indians. At this time, Portolá journeyed among the Chumash and

Missions at Santa Barbara and elsewhere in California came to dominate the Chumash and other native peoples who lived in the region.

Mission Santa Ynez was established in the heart of Chumash territory, not far from the present-day reservation and the town of Solvang.

reported that they were friendly and offered gifts of baskets, fish, seeds, and acorns. However, the Spanish intended to use the Chumash and other California natives as slave laborers to enrich their empire. Although many of the missionaries hoped to better the lives of the Chumash, some were very cruel. Whatever the priests' motives, the traditional life of the Chumash began to be destroyed when the missions were established in their homeland.

In 1772, the Spanish established San Luis Obispo, the first of the five missions in Chumash territory: San Luis Obispo, San Buenaventura (at Ventura), Santa Barbara, La Purísima Concepción (near Lompoc), and Santa Ynez. Completed in 1804, Santa Ynez Mission was the last of the missions to be built on Chumash land. The priests hoped to convert the Indians to Christianity. The Chumash were lured to the missions by attractive trade beads.

Some terrified people fled to the missions after a major earthquake in 1812. Many Chumash on the Channel Islands were slaughtered by Russian whalers, and the survivors made their way to the missions. They willingly adapted to a new way of life as farmers, craftsmen, and Christians. However, most were forced to work on the missions. They and other native peoples associated with the missions in California came to be known as Mission Indians. Eventually, their villages declined so much that it was impossible to survive in traditional communities, and most Chumash people had to enter the mission system.

Once the Chumash had been baptized they were regarded as neophytes. According to Spanish law, neophytes had to abandon their villages and live near the mission. At the age of five or six, children of the neophytes were taken from their parents and forced to live in dormitories. They had to attend religious services conducted in Spanish and their own native language. The Chumash also had to give up their traditional dress and wear woolen clothing made at the mission. Children learned farming, carpentry, masonry, ironworking, pottery, weaving, and other crafts. Hunting, fishing, and gathering were abandoned in favor of agriculture and trades. People worked without pay. Instead of dome-shaped tule houses, they now lived in rectangular adobe rooms. Though ravaged by this mistreatment, the peaceful Chumash did not openly resist any of these regulations. To do otherwise would risk severe punishment—beatings, imprisonment, and backbreaking labor.

Although the Chumash had initially welcomed the Spanish, they suffered terribly under their harsh rule. But the Chumash and the other native California peoples were even more devastated by smallpox, measles, and other European diseases that swept through the missions. They had little or no resistance to these diseases, and young children were especially susceptible. The worst was a measles epidemic in the winter of 1806, which killed many people along the California coast. Alcoholism soon became a devastating problem for California Indians, including the Chumash. The population of the Chumash went into sharp decline once the Spanish arrived.

When the Mexican government, which had won independence from Spain in 1821, took control of California, the missions were severely hampered by a lack of supplies. The Chumash rebelled against the mission system at Santa Ynez, La Purísima, and Santa Barbara in 1824. Neophytes from Santa Barbara and Santa Ynez then abandoned their missions and joined with the rebels at La Purísima. The Chumash held the mission for more than a month, but surrendered when confronted by troops equipped with cannons. Some Chumash fled to the mountains and others sought refuge among the Yokuts and other native people living farther inland. However, the revolts quickly ended and many Chumash returned to the missions.

In 1833, the Mexican government began to dismantle the missions, and the vast land holdings passed from the Catholic Church to Mexican landowners. The Mexicans freed the Chumash and promised to return a portion of their lands. However, the Chumash

Military forts, known as presidios, were established near the missions to enforce rule over the Chumash and other native peoples.

As they adapted to the culture of the newcomers, the Chumash abandoned many of their traditional beliefs and customs.

never received any of their former territory. The missions no longer provided a livelihood and ancestral Chumash lands were now owned by wealthy Mexicans. A few people tried farming for themselves, but they were driven from the land and enslaved by the settlers who were pouring into the territory from Mexico. Many worked long hours as servants or ranch hands for little or no wages on large ranches. A few people sought work in Los Angeles and the other towns growing along the coast, and some fled to the interior to live with the Yokuts and the Kitanemuk.

Within a few decades, the Chumash were nearly wiped out. By 1839, only about 250 native people remained at Santa Barbara Mission.

In 1848, Mexico ceded California to the United States, and the last of Chumash lands were seized by Americans. Gold was discovered in northern California and thousands of settlers poured into California, hoping to get rich not only as gold prospectors, but also as farmers, ranchers, and merchants. Even more settlers arrived after California became a state in 1850. The newcomers either feared or pitied the impoverished Chumash. There were no laws to protect the Chumash, and they were driven from their few remaining villages. People scattered throughout the region, afraid to admit that they were Chumash. As Chumash children learned Spanish and English, the Chumash languages were abandoned. Unable to find jobs, many lived in poverty, as outcasts in their own land.

Despite these many hardships, a few Chumash struggled to preserve some remnants of their traditional life. Wots were still selected as late as 1862 when Pomposa, a Chumash woman, became chief of the Ventura Indians at the town of Saticoy. In 1869, she gave the last traditional ceremony. Fernando Librado, who spent most of his early years at San Buenaventura Mission, devoted most of his life to learning about Chumash traditions, handicrafts, stories, and songs. He visited many elders and tried to learn as much as possible about traditional beliefs and practices. When he was an old man, Fernando shared much of this knowledge with John P. Harrington, who preserved these traditions through various writings.

One Chumash community did manage to survive the challenges of change. In 1855, the U.S. government attempted to help the Chumash by setting aside a parcel of 120 acres for a little more than 100 Chumash people living near the Santa Ynez Mission. This land became the only reservation for the Chumash. Officially known as the Santa Ynez Chumash Reservation, this reservation was reduced in size in 1901, to become the smallest in California. Most of the few remaining Chumash lived in Ventura or Santa Barbara or on ranches where they worked as shepherds, cowboys, laborers, or servants.

Chumash Language

California had the greatest number of languages of any region in North America. Chumash, or Chumashan, though possibly related to some of the other California languages, is now considered a language family all to itself, including at least six separate languages: Ventureño, Barbareño, Ynezeño, Purisimeño, Obispeño, and Island Chumash. Because the groups speaking these languages lived in relative isolation from each other for thousands of years, distinct languages developed. Members of each group could not understand the language of any of its neighbors.

The Spanish nearly wiped out the Chumash by the early 1800s. When the United States took over California, English gradually replaced the native languages. By the beginning of the twentieth century, Spanish or English was spoken in most California households. Throughout the early to mid-1900s, children learned English in public schools. Only a few individuals learned their native languages as they grew up. Those born before 1900 remembered their own language, but it vanished as their elders passed away. The last known native speaker of Barbareño, Mary J. Yee, died in 1964.

Here are some examples of the Barbareño Chumash language based on *An Interim Barbareño Chumash Dictionary* as spoken by Mary Yee and compiled by Kenneth W. Whistler in 1980. Chumash is complex and the following examples have been simplified. The vowels and the consonants may be pronounced as in English. Chumash pronunciation includes the glottal stop, a catch-in-the-breath expression, similar to the stop in "oh-oh." A glottal stop is indicated by an apostrophe (').

People and Daily Life

acorn	'ixpanish
arrow	ya'
aunt	ha'wa
brother, older	'a'mi
canoe	tomol
ceremony leader	paha
chief	wot'
child	ch'ish'i
daughter	sha'y
good-bye	kiwa'nan
grandchild	'u'nu
grandfather	nono
grandmother	ne'ne
hello	haku
house	'ap
man	'ihi'y
messenger	ksen
religious society	'antap
sacred enclosure	siliyik
singer	'a'lalexpech
sister	'amut'ey
sister, older	'a'mi
son	wop
talisman	'atashwin
uncle	tat'a
woman	'eneq

Parts of the Body

arm	pu, wach'ax
ear	tu'
elbow	shipuk
eye	tiq
finger, toe	mimi
foot	'i'l, 'eqe'ne
hand	pu
head	noqsh, 'oqwo'n
heart	'ayapis, 'antik, ahash
knee	istukun
shoulder	qe'nen
skin	pax

Natural World

beach	muhuw, xasxas'
cliff	shi
island	'enemes, naxalamuw
lightning	squnt'aw
land	shup
shore	muhuw, pana'yi'w
sky	'alapay
star	'aqiwo
sun	'alishaw
valley	stawayik'

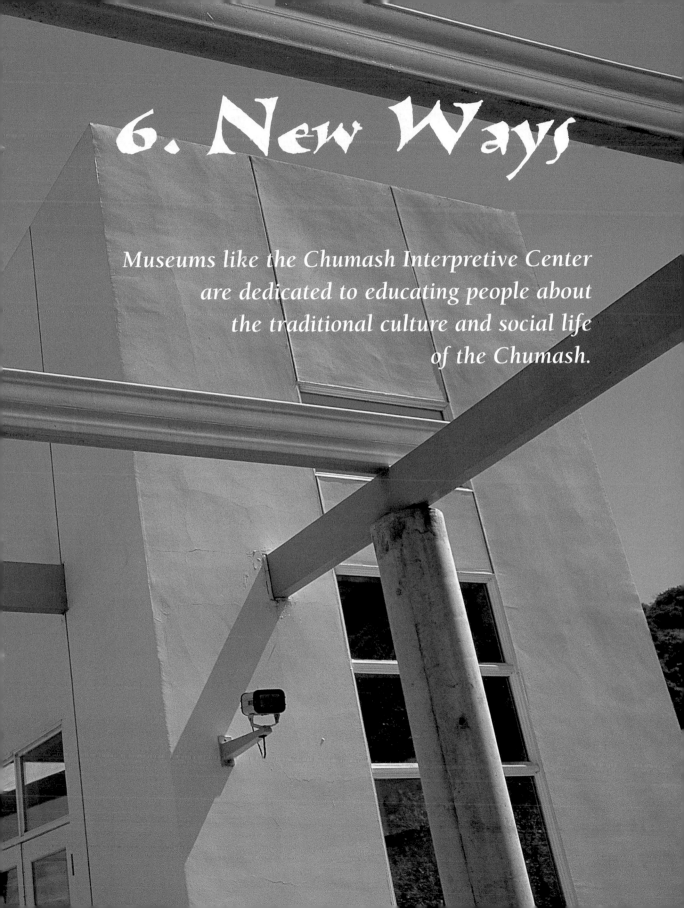

6. New Ways

Museums like the Chumash Interpretive Center
are dedicated to educating people about
the traditional culture and social life
of the Chumash.

BY THE BEGINNING OF THE TWENTIETH CENTURY, EVERY CHUMASH VILLAGE except one had been abandoned. Somehow, a small group of Chumash managed to survive as a community along Zanja de Cota Creek near Santa Ynez Mission. In 1855, the United States granted land to the Chumash living in this area, and in 1901, the government formally established a reservation here. Although the reservation is small, it is now the home of the only federally recognized Chumash tribe in the United States. Only those people living at Zanja de Cota were allowed to enroll as members of the tribe at Santa Ynez. The remaining Chumash lived alone or in small families in Ventura, Santa Barbara, and San Luis Obispo Counties in southern California.

By the early 1900s, most Chumash were of mixed ancestry because of intermarriage with other California Indians, and with Mexicans, Mexican-Americans, and Americans. Over the past hundred years, the number of Chumash has steadily grown. Compiled between 1968 and 1972, the California Indian Judgment Roll listed 1,925 people as Chumash. Of these people, 865 were then living in the three counties that once comprised most of Chumash territory. It is estimated that there are now about 5,000 Chumash people, about 1,500 of whom live in central California.

In recent years, only a small number of Chumash people have lived on the reservation. The 1940 census of the Santa Ynez Reservation, used to determine the voting membership, counted just over 150 people. People must have at least one-fourth "degree of blood" to become tribal members. The reservation has grown from four house-

The Chumash reservation at Santa Ynez provides important housing, education, and health services to community members.

holds in the 1930s to eighty-one households and 320 residents today. Since 1977, three Housing and Urban Development grants have enabled the reservation to provide homes for many families moving to Santa Ynez. New homes continue to be built in both the upper and the lower villages on the reservation.

As provided in the 1968 Articles of Incorporation, the Chumash at Santa Ynez are represented by their own five-member Business Council. Over the years, the reservation has grown slightly to 127 acres. A tribal hall was erected in 1976. A health clinic provides medical care and offers substance abuse programs funded by county and federal agencies. A campground and a thriving bingo casino, both established in 1994, provide employment for tribal members and revenue for reservation programs.

The Chumash have fought for recognition in other ways, too. In May 1978, about twenty-five Chumash people took part in a three-day protest at an ancient burial site at Little Cohu Bay, Point Conception, California. A facility for importing liquefied natural gas was planned for this site. However, an agreement was reached in which the Chumash were allowed to visit the area for religious ceremonies. All ruins and artifacts at the site are to be protected and six tribal members are to monitor all future excavations.

The Chumash are striving to overcome many obstacles. Although their one reservation is quite small, new houses are being constructed to support more families. Scattered throughout southern California, off-reservation Chumash have formed groups to preserve their heritage. In recent years, there has been a resurgence in Chumash culture

*E*ven as they adopt new ways, Chumash children are also learning about the rich history of their ancestors.

spurred in part by research and programs at museums and schools. Traditions are sustained at public events that include dances, songs, and storytelling. Workshops in basket weaving, beadwork, and canoe building are held so that future generations may learn the skill and artistry of their Chumash ancestors. Efforts are being made to protect sacred shrines and burial places.

Today, the Chumash are proud of their history and heritage. As they struggle to make a home for themselves, they look forward to a bright and prosperous future for their children and grandchildren.

More about

the Chumash

Timeline

9000–6000 B.C.   Early people live in small bands, harvesting shellfish and hunting game. They use stone tools, make baskets, and fashion bead jewelry. The climate is cool and moist, with sprawling pine forests.

6000–3000 B.C.   Subsistence activities shift to gathering seeds. This time is known as The Milling Stone Period because of the abundance of milling stones (metates and manos) used to grind acorns and the small, hard seeds of grasses that are a principal food. Human population increases. Hunters begin to use the atlatl to hunt elk, deer, and sea mammals. People speak an early Chumash language in the Santa Barbara region.

3000–800 B.C.   Fishing with shell hooks and barbed harpoons and hunting sea mammals becomes more important. The tomol is adopted around 2000 B.C. More abundant fishing leads to the growth of large, permanent villages on the coast. Around 1500 B.C., the bow and arrow replaces the atlatl. Warfare increases during a period of drought.

800 B.C.–A.D. 1772   Marine fishing using nets remains a major source of Chumash subsistence. Hunting and gathering wild plants, notably acorns and various seeds, supplement the seafood diet. Two-thirds of the Chumash people live near the coast. People use shell beads, produced mostly on the northern Channel Islands, as money. Trade and warfare become important.

1772   San Luis Obispo is the first of the Spanish missions to be built in Chumash territory.

1772–1822   Traditions of hunting, fishing, and gathering are abandoned in favor of cultivation of crops and raising livestock.

1824   Chumash rise up against the mission system at Santa Ynez, La Purísima, and Santa Barbara.

1833   The Mexican government transfers the land holdings of the missions from the Catholic Church to Mexican landowners.

1848   Mexico cedes California to the United States, and the remaining Chumash lands are taken by Americans. Gold is discovered in California.

1849   The California Gold Rush draws thousands of settlers to California.

1850   California becomes a state and more settlers flood into traditional Chumash territory.

1901   The Santa Ynez Reservation, the smallest in California and the only Chumash reservation, is established.

1978   The Chumash agree to end a three-day protest at one of their ancient burial sites.

1994   A bingo casino is established on the Santa Ynez Reservation to provide a source of tribal income.

2002   Construction of new buildings for a tribal hall and a health clinic on the Santa Ynez Reservation is planned.

Notable People

Juan de Jesús Justo (1858–1941), storyteller and ethnohistorian, was born in the Santa Barbara area ten years after the United States acquired California from Mexico. Juan's father was known as Old Justo. At the time, the Chumash had already suffered greatly—first from the Spanish and Mexicans and then from the Americans who seized ancestral lands and forced the Chumash to abandon their way of life. Yet Juan's father refused to abandon the traditional practices and beliefs of his people. Old Justo worked with scholars such as Oscar Loew and Henry Henshaw to preserve Chumash vocabulary and identify place names. As Juan grew up, his father and his mother Cecilia made certain that he learned about his heritage.

Juan became well known as a storyteller and an expert on Chumash culture having a lively and colorful personality. Working with ethnohistorian John P. Harrington and Alfred Kroeber, he became central in preserving Chumash history and culture in published documents, sound recordings, photographs, and motion pictures. He was also considered an authority on the Mexican influence on the Chumash people. In 1914, he served as an actor in a film produced by Harrington and Kroeber. Juan provided many of the Chumash stories that Harrington collected in *December's Child*, a book that has made a major contribution in understanding and preserving Chumash culture. In the late 1930s, Juan worked with Harrington's nephew to make sound recordings of Chumash language in the years before his death in 1941.

Kitsepawit (Fernando Librado) (1839–1915) was born in the seaport of Swaxil on Santa Cruz Island. His paternal grandfather was the leader of the village. His father, grandfather, and great-grandfather were all named Kitsepawit, and each of them resisted both the Spanish and the Mexicans. The Island Chumash were devastated by plagues and attacks by Aleuts working for the Russians in the otter trade. The remaining villagers, mostly

Juan de Jesús Justo

Fernando Librado

women and children, fled to San Buenaventura Mission on the mainland. Here, Kitsepawit was raised by his mother who taught him the language of the island. When forced to adopt a Mexican name, he chose Librado from the Spanish "libertador," which means "liberator."

Kitsepawit always identified with his Chumash ancestry and devoted his life to learning about his heritage, even though he had to live under the mission system. By 1845, the Mission Indians were left destitute. The California Gold Rush then brought waves of settlers into the region. Kitsepawit lived in poverty in the Mexican community in Ventura but finally moved to the mountains to work as a sheepherder and ranch hand. During this time, he frequently visited Chumash families and gained valuable knowledge about the traditional lands, village sites, and sacred places of his people.

In his later years, Kitsepawit became friends with John P. Harrington, an anthropologist working with the Smithsonian Institution. Before he died in 1915, Kitsepawit provided Harrington with a wealth of knowledge about Chumash language, culture, and history that would otherwise have been lost.

Pacomio (active 1820s) was brought up and educated by the padres at La Purísima Mission located between Santa Barbara and San Luis Obispo. He became a highly skilled carpenter, but hated Spanish domination. Angry about the mistreatment of his people, he organized a revolt of the Mission Indians to drive the Spanish from California. He traveled to other missions to encourage the Indians living there to support the uprising. He also convinced neighboring tribes, such as the Yokuts, to move close to the missions to facilitate a surprise attack.

On the day of the uprising, Pacomio sent messengers to inform his allies. Some messengers reached the missions at Santa Barbara and Santa Ynez. However, those going to the northern missions were caught. On March 19, 1824, believed to be the day planned for the attack, Pacomio declared himself to be chief of all the native peoples of California. He led a force of about 2,000 men against La Purísima, captured the mission, and jailed the soldiers. The native people at Santa Barbara and Santa Ynez also revolted. However, other Mission Indians did not join the uprising and the Spanish soon counterattacked. The rebellion gradually ended and Pacomio surrendered. He was allowed to live peacefully at Monterey, but little else is known about this brave man.

Maria Solares (about 1842–1922), was born near the Santa Ynez Mission and lived in that area for her entire life. She was educated in both the traditional Chumash way of life and the Catholic mission system. Her father Benvenuto Qililkutayiwit and paternal grandparents were both from the village of Kalawasaq, located close to the mission. However, by the 1880s, the village had been abandoned as priests moved the inhabitants into housing near the mission. Maria married Manual Solares whose father Raphael Solares was the last person to serve as a Chumash religious leader.

Maria's mother Brigada, who was half-Chumash and half-Yokut, was born in the Yokut village of Tinlew just south of present-day Bakersfield. When Brigada was dying in 1868, she asked Maria to visit her Yokut and Chumash relatives. Years later, Maria worked with ethnologist and linguist John P. Harrington to record a personal account of her visit. These narratives recounted the experiences of her uncle Juan Moynal, who served as mayor of Tinlew, and her traditionalist uncle Sapakay, who never lived among Christian peoples. Maria is regarded as one of John P. Harrington's important sources of information about the Chumash.

Glossary

adobe   Bricks and building material made of sun-dried mud and straw; also the name of buildings made with this material.

'antap   A Chumash religious society.

'ap   A Chumash dwelling made of poles covered with tule and cattails.

channel   A narrow body of water separating two land masses.

mission   A religious community centered around a church.

padre   The Spanish name for a priest of the Catholic Church.

paha   A ceremonial leader responsible for making speeches and managing dancing and singing at fiestas.

pictograph   A sign or symbol drawn or painted on a rock, cliff, or cave wall.

shaman   A religious leader responsible for the spiritual and physical well-being of the people.

siliyik   A dance space used at special times during the year.

solstice   The two times in the year (winter and summer) when the sun is farthest north or south of the equator.

temascal   The Spanish word for a Chumash sweathouse. Also spelled *temescal*.

toloache   A hallucinogenic drink made from jimsonweed that was taken during religious ceremonies to induce dreams.

tomol   A canoe made from wooden planks sewn together.

wot   The chief who held the highest position in Chumash society.

Further Information

Readings

Many excellent books have been published about the Chumash. In preparing this book, the following books for children and adults were consulted. *The Chumash People: Materials for Teachers and Students* prepared by Lynne McCall, Rosalind Perry, and others is particularly recommended to children and educators who would like to learn more about the Chumash.

The two stories included in this book are adapted from stories collected by John Harrington and published in *December's Child: A Book of Chumash Oral Narratives*.

Anderson, Eugene N. *The Chumash Indians of Southern California.* Banning, CA: Malki Museum Press, 1968.

Arnold, Jeanne E. *The Origins of a Pacific Coast Chiefdom: the Chumash of the Channel Islands.* Salt Lake City: University of Utah Press, 2001.

The Encyclopedia of North American Indians. New York: Marshall Cavendish, 1997.

Grant, Campbell. *The Rock Paintings of the Chumash: A Study of a California Indian Culture.* Santa Barbara, CA: Santa Barbara Museum of Natural History; San Luis Obispo, CA: EZ Nature Books, 1993.

Harrington, John Peabody, and Thomas C. Blackburn. *December's Child: A Book of Chumash Oral Narratives.* Berkeley: University of California Press, 1975, 1980.

Holmes, Marie S., and John R. Johnson. *The Chumash and Their Predecessors: An Annotated Bibliography.* Santa Barbara, CA: Santa Barbara Museum of Natural History, 1998.

Hudson, Travis, and Janice Timbrook. *Chumash Indian Games.* Santa Barbara, CA: Santa Barbara Museum of Natural History, 1997.

Hudson, Travis. *Chumash Wooden Bowls, Trays and Boxes.* San Diego, CA: San Diego Museum of Man, 1977.

Hudson, Travis, and Thomas C. Blackburn. *The Material Culture of the Chumash Interaction Sphere.* Los Altos, CA: Ballena Press; Santa Barbara, CA: Santa Barbara Museum of Natural History, 1982–1987.

Johansen, Bruce E., and Donald A. Grinde Jr. *The Encyclopedia of Native American Biography.* New York: Henry Holt, 1997.

King, Chester. *Evolution of Chumash Society: A Comparative Study of Artifacts Used for Social System Maintenance in the Santa Barbara Channel Region Before A. D. 1804.* New York: Garland Publishing, 1990.

Langer, Howard J., editor. *American Indian Quotations.* Westport, CT: Greenwood Press, 1996.

Lee, Georgia. *The Chumash Cosmos: Effigies, Ornaments, Incised Stones and Rock Paintings of the Chumash Indians.* Arroyo Grande, CA: Bear Flag Books, 1997.

Librado, Fernando. *Breath of the Sun: Life in Early California.* Banning, CA: Malki Museum Press; Ventura County Historical Society, 1979, 1980.

Librado, Fernando. *The Eye of the Flute: Chumash Traditional History and Ritual.* Banning, CA: Malki Museum Press; Santa Barbara, CA: Santa Barbara Museum of Natural History, 1981.

McCall, Lynne, and Rosalind Perry. *The Chumash People: Materials for Teachers and Students.* Revised edition. San Luis Obispo, CA: EZ Nature, 1991, 1982.

Malinowski, Sharon, and Anna Sheets. *The Gale Encyclopedia of Native American Tribes*. Detroit: Gale Research, 1998.

Malinowski, Sharon. *Notable Native Americans*. New York: Gale Research, 1995.

Olson, Ronald L. *Chumash Prehistory*. New York: Kraus, 1965.

Perry, Rosalind. *California's Chumash Indians: A Project of the Santa Barbara Museum of Natural History Education Center*. San Luis Obispo, CA: EZ Nature Books, 1996, 1986.

Pritzker, Barry M. *Native Americans: an Encyclopedia of History, Culture, and Peoples*. Santa Barbara, CA: ABC-CLIO, 1998.

Richie, C. F., and R. A. Hager. *The Chumash Canoe: The Structure and Hydrodynamics of a Model*. San Diego, CA: San Diego Museum of Man, 1973.

Sanger, Kay. *When the Animals Were People: Stories Told by the Chumash Indians of California*. Banning, CA: Malki Museum Press, 1983.

Walker, Phillip L. and Travis Hudson. *Chumash Healing: Changing Health and Medical Practices in an American Indian Society*. Banning, CA: Malki Museum Press, 1993.

Whitley, David S.; Ellen L. McCann; and C. William Clewlow Jr. *Inland Chumash Archaeological Investigations*. Los Angeles: Institute of Archaeology, University of California, Los Angeles, 1980.

Children's Books

Behrens, June. *Missions of the Central Coast*. Minneapolis: Lerner Publications, 1996.

Boulé, Mary Null, and Liddell, Daniel. *California Native American Tribes: Chumash*. Vashon, WA: Merryant Publishing, 1992.

Brower, Pauline. *Missions of the Inland Valleys.* Minneapolis: Lerner Publications, 1996.

Ching, Jacqueline. *Mission Santa Inés.* New York: PowerKids Press, 2000.

Duvall, Jill. *The Chumash.* Chicago: Childrens Press, 1994.

Edgar, Kathleen J., and Susan E. Edgar. *Mission of San Luis Obispo de Tolosa.* New York: PowerKids Press, 2000.

Fraser, Mary Ann. *A Mission for the People: The Story of La Purisima.* New York: Henry Holt, 1997.

Gibson, Robert O. *The Chumash.* New York: Chelsea House Publishers, 1991.

Lee, Georgia. *A Day With a Chumash.* Minneapolis: Runestone Press, 1999.

Lund, Bill. *The Chumash Indians.* Mankato, MN: Capstone Press, 1998.

MacMillan, Dianne M. *Missions of the Los Angeles Area.* Minneapolis, MN: Lerner Publications, 1996.

Margaret, Amy. *Mission Santa Bárbara.* New York: PowerKids Press, 2000.

Margaret, Amy. *Mission San Buenaventura.* New York: PowerKids Press, 2000.

McGinty, Alice B. *Mission San Gabriel Arcángel.* New York: PowerKids Press, 2000.

Ostrow, Kim. *Mission La Purísima Concepción.* New York: PowerKids Press, 2000.

Schwabacher, Martin. *The Chumash Indians.* New York: Chelsea Juniors, 1995.

Wilcox, John. *The Chumash: Through a Child's Eyes.* Santa Barbara, CA: Shoreline Press, 1997.

Wood, Audrey. *The Rainbow Bridge: Inspired by a Chumash Tale.* San Diego: Harcourt Brace Jovanovich, 1995.

Young, Robert. *A Personal Tour of La Purísima.* Minneapolis: Lerner Publications, 1999.

Organizations

The California Indian Museum and Cultural Center

5250 Aero Drive

Santa Rosa, CA 95403

Phone: (707) 579-3004

Fax: (707) 579-3351

Chumash Interpretive Center and Museum

3290 Lang Ranch Parkway

Thousand Oaks, CA 91362

Phone: (805) 492-8076

Fax: (805) 492-7996

Santa Barbara Museum of Natural History

2559 Puesta de Sol Road

Santa Barbara, CA 93105

Phone: (805) 682-4711

Fax: (805) 569-3170

Santa Ynez Reservation

P. O. Box 517

Santa Ynez, CA 93460

Phone: (805) 688-7997

Fax: (805) 688-8005

Web Sites

The Barbareno Chumash Indian Council
http://expage.com/barbara44

The California Indian Museum and Cultural Center
http://cimcc.indian.com/

The Chumash Indian Council of San Luis Obispo County
(Southern California)
http://www.angelfire.com/id/newpubs/slo.html

Chumash Indian Life: Santa Barbara Museum of Natural History
http://www.sbnature.org/research/anthro/chumash/

The Chumash Indians: Native People of Southern California
http://expage.com/page/chumashindians

The Chumash Indians of the Los Angeles Region
http://expage.com/chumashla44

The Chumash Indians Who Live in Ventura County California
http://www.angelfire.com/id/newpubs/ven77.html

The Chumash Islanders
http://expage.com/page/chumashislanders

Coastal Band of the Chumash Nation
http://expage.com/page/coastal46

Dolphin Clan Chumash
http://dolphinclan.gq.nu/

The Kagismuwas
http://john888.freeyellow.com/kagis.html

Chumash Council of Bakersfield
http://expage.com/page/jamesleon

Malki Museum
http://www.malkimuseum.org/

Oakbrook Regional Park: Chumash Interpretive Center
http://www.designplace.com/chumash/

The San Fernando Valley Chumash: Native Peoples of Southern California
http://expage.com/page/tongva55

Tejon Indians: Native Peoples of Southern California
http://expage.com/page/tejonres

Wishtoyo Foundation
http://www.wishtoyo.org

Index

Page numbers in **boldface** are illustrations.

map, 12

adultery, 31
agriculture, 38, 90, 108
alcoholism, 91
Aleuts, 110–113
alliances, 29
ancestors, 13, 66, 108
animals, 72
anthropologists. *See* Harrington, John P.;
    Kroeber, Alfred
ants, 70
art. *See* crafts; rock paintings
artisans, 30, **32–33**, 56
    boat-builders, 45–48
astronomy, 66

baskets, 56–63, **59**, **62**
beliefs, 10, 30, **64–65**, 66–68, **67**
    See also legends; rock paintings
birth, 34
body painting, 31, 51, 55, 72
body piercing, 55

canoes, 44–48, **46–47**
carving, 51, 56
Channel Islands, **12**, 14–18
chiefs, 24, 26, 28, 29, 55, 68, 95–96
    relatives of, 30
children, 34–36, 76, 90, 91, **105**
    naming, 30
clans, 30–31, 36
clothing, **12**, **53**, 53–55, 68, **85**, 90, **94**
Coastal Chumash, 11–13, 18, 26
coming-of-age, 36
cooking, 24, 42, 60

councils, 29
    contemporary, 121, 122
Coyote, 10–11, 81
crafts, **35**, 39, 55–63, **57**, **59**, **61**, **62**, 105
    See also canoes; decorations
cultural preservation, 95–96, 104–105,
    110–114

dances, 36–37, 72, 105
death, 28, 37, 66, 104–105
debts, 71
decorations, 51, **54**, 55
disputes, 22
dream helpers, 68
dreams, 30
drinks, 42, 70
    hallucinogenic, 36, 68

education, 34–36, 80, 95
elderly, 29
entertainment, 28
Europeans
    diseases, 91, 110
    explorers, 86
    forts, **92–93**
    missions, 86–95, **87**, **88–89**, 108
    Russians, 90, 110–113

families, 24–26, 36–37, 102
festivals, 70
fishing, 38, 40–41, 58, 90, 108
fishing rights, 29
food, 28, 29, 36, 38–42, **41**, 108
furniture, 26, 56

gambling, 76, 81–83, 104, 109
games, 28, 76–80, **77**, **78–79**
gathering, 10, 38, 41, **41**, 90, 108

Raymond Bial

HAS PUBLISHED MORE THAN THIRTY CRITICALLY ACCLAIMED BOOKS OF photographs for children and adults. His photo-essays for children include *Corn Belt Harvest, Amish Home, Frontier Home, Shaker Home, The Underground Railroad, Portrait of a Farm Family, With Needle and Thread: A Book About Quilts, Mist Over the Mountains: Appalachia and Its People, Cajun Home,* and *Where Lincoln Walked.*

He is currently immersed in writing *Lifeways,* a series of books about Native Americans. As with his other work, Bial's deep feeling for his subjects is evident in both the text and illustrations. He travels to tribal cultural centers, photographing homes, artifacts, and surroundings and learning firsthand about the national lifeways of these peoples.

A full-time library director at a small college in Champaign, Illinois, he lives with his wife and three children in nearby Urbana.